W9-AUJ-925

Drones

BY KIRSTEN W. LARSON

AMICUS HIGH INTEREST • AMICUS INK

Amicus High Interest and Amicus Ink are imprints of Amicus
P.O. Box 1329, Mankato, MN 56002
www.amicuspublishing.us

Library of Congress Cataloging-in-Publication Data
Names: Larson, Kirsten W., author.
Title: Drones / by Kirsten W. Larson.
Description: Mankato, Minnesota : Amicus High Interest/
  Amicus Ink, [2018] | Series: Robotics in our world |
  Audience: Grades 4 to 6. | Includes bibliographical
  references and index.
Identifiers: LCCN 2016034046 (print) | LCCN 2016039198
  (ebook) | ISBN 9781681511405 (library binding : alk.
  paper) | ISBN 9781681521718 (pbk. : alk. paper) | ISBN
  9781681512303 (ebook) | ISBN 9781681512303 (pdf)
Subjects: LCSH: Drone aircraft–Juvenile literature. | Robotics–
  Juvenile literature.
Classification: LCC UG1242.D7 L37 2018 (print) | LCC
  UG1242.D7 (ebook) | DDC 623.74/69–dc23
LC record available at https://lccn.loc.gov/2016034046

Editor: Wendy Dieker
Series Designer: Kathleen Petelinsek
Book Designer: Tracy Myers
Photo Researcher: Holly Young

Photo Credits: US Air Force Photo/Alamy Stock Photo cover;
Martin UAV 5; Nicole Franco/NF 6-7; seregalsv/Shutterstock
9; U.S. Navy circa 1944-1946/WikiCommons 10; George
Stroud/Stringer/Collection: Hulton Archive/Getty 13; Michael
Pereckas/CC BY 2.0/WikiCommons 14; Cyril Ndegeya/
AFP/Getty 17; Stanislav Komogorov/libertos/123RF Stock
Photo/123RF 18-19; John Moore/Staff/Getty Images News/
Getty 21; bibiphoto/Shutterstock 22; Provided by Flirtey 25;
Boeing Images 26; Getty 29

Printed in the United States of America

HC 10 9 8 7 6 5 4 3 2 1
PB 10 9 8 7 6 5 4 3 2 1

The author thanks NASA Armstrong Chief Pilot Nils Larson for his assistance with this book.

Table of Contents

The Drone Ranger

A tiny plane flies over a herd of rhinos. Using its cameras, it scans for **poachers**. Poachers kill rhinos for their horns. When the plane spots a poacher, it alerts park rangers. They drive to the site. They get the bad guys. Gotcha! But where is the pilot? He is not in the plane. This plane is a drone.

 How does the drone alert rangers?

This robot plane carries cameras and watches for poachers in Africa.

 **A** It sends a signal to a ground station. Rangers watch the drone's flight from there.

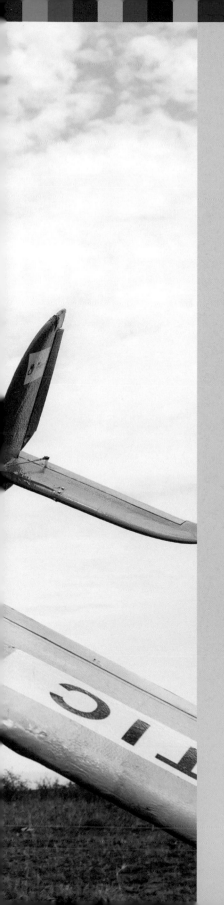

A drone is a robot. Like all robots, a drone is a machine that can do work by itself. A person tells the drone's computer where to fly. Then he launches the drone like a paper airplane. The drone decides the best way to reach the herd. It steers itself. Rangers on the ground can see pictures the drone sends back.

A man gets ready to launch a drone over a herd.

7

Drones are planes that have jobs to do. Some might catch poachers. Others drop bombs. Yet not all drones fly themselves. Some need pilots. But where do the pilots sit? They stay on the ground. They use handheld controllers, computers, or even smart phones to fly the drone. If the pilot cannot tell the drone what to do, the drones can often fly themselves.

Is my remote control model airplane a drone?

Drones can do some tasks on their own. But a person still has to control many of them.

 No. Aircraft under 55 pounds (25 kg) flown just for fun are not drones. Drones have jobs to do. And they can fly themselves at times.

In the 1940s, the navy also used
remote control bombs.

Early Drones

Drones started as a way to keep pilots safe. During World War II (1939–45), pilots dropped bombs from planes. Enemies shot these planes out of the sky. The crews died. The U.S. Army started using old planes as drones. They did not have pilots inside, but they were loaded up with bombs. Pilots in other planes used a remote control to fly the drones into targets. Then the drone blew up. Boom!

The airplane drones the army used in World War II had video cameras inside. The pilot could see the control panel on video. He could also see out the window. He used a remote to steer the drone. Other early drones used **autopilot**. These drones could steer themselves. Using a special **compass**, a person set the drone's course. The autopilot steered the drone. No pilot needed!

An early autopilot control panel like this could steer planes on its own.

How Drones Work

Flying a plane without a pilot inside seems crazy. But modern technology makes it work. On a normal plane, the pilot looks out for storms. When she spots one, she steers away from it. But drones have **sensors**. These work like a pilot's eyes and ears. They watch for trees and buildings. Then computers make decisions. The computer steers the drone. It doesn't crash.

A system of cameras and sensors is on the front of a drone behind small windows.

Many drones use **GPS**. This system tells a drone where it is in the world. First, a person tells the drone's computer where to go. Using GPS, the drone finds the best route. Then it flies there by itself. All the while, a camera can take pictures of the land. Then the drone flies home again.

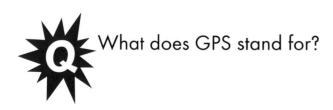 What does GPS stand for?

A drone's pilot uses a phone to set the place where the drone should go. The drone sends video back.

 It stands for Global Positioning System.

Radio control is another key technology. A pilot's controller sends radio signals to the drone. The drone sends signals back. The two can "talk." Over long distances, **satellites** help them talk. If the radio link is lost, drones may circle and wait. Will the link come back? No? If not, some drones will fly home and land. Wow!

Many drones use a mix of radio control and robot technology.

The U.S. Air Force uses large drones. Large drones often use radio control. The *Predator* is a spy drone. It can also launch missiles. A pilot sits at a station on the ground. His plane may be on the other side of the world. But the pilot can see where the drone is on video screens. He uses a joystick to fly the drone to the target.

 A pilot flies this drone. Is the *Predator* a robot?

A worker checks the *Predator* drone. This robotic plane has many jobs.

 Yes. It has sensors and a computer. It can fly home by itself if it needs to.

A drone with a camera flies above homes. What does it see? Does it see you?

 Q Can drones take off on their own? Or shoot missiles on their own?

Future Drones

Are drones good or bad? Some people think drones are good and helpful. Other people worry about too many drones in the air. Drones could crash into other planes. Others fear drones are spying on them.

In the U.S., the Federal Aviation Administration (FAA) decides where and when drones can fly. The FAA makes sure the skies stay safe.

 No. People need to program their computers. Drones can only do what people tell them to do.

Some companies are working to use drones for deliveries. Flirtey is one company that is leading the way. In November 2016, Flirtey drones started carrying food, drinks, and medicine to homes from a store. Amazon.com is making drone deliveries in the United Kingdom. Companies like these hope to show the FAA that drone deliveries can be safe.

 Can Flirtey bring goods to my home?

Someday a drone might carry a package to your door.

 Maybe! You need to live close enough to a store that delivers by drone. At this time, a drone operator has to be able to see the drone at all times during its flight.

This drone could stay in the air for four days. It could send cell signals or map a disaster area.

 Is this long-flying drone a robot?

Today cell towers on the ground send your phone calls and texts. But what if an earthquake knocks down the towers? Drones with cell antennas might help. They could relay the signals. Boeing built a drone that is up to the task. Its special engine can fly for four days. The drone can send signals across 400 nautical miles (741 kilometers).

 Yes. A person on the ground tells it where to fly. The drone does the rest on its own.

A World of Drones

We face a future filled with drones. Drones help animals. They spy on enemies and help fight wars. More and more people fly them for fun. In the future, drones might fill the skies. They could deliver your next book or snack. Who knows what else drones will do? These flying robots will change our world.

The *MQ9-Reaper* does many jobs for the U.S. Air Force with no pilot inside.

Glossary

autopilot A system for automatically controlling an airplane, ship, or spacecraft.

compass An instrument that shows which direction—north, south, east, or west—something is going or pointing.

GPS Short for Global Positioning System; a network of satellites that sends information about a device's location on earth.

poacher A person who hunts or fishes illegally.

radio A way of communicating that uses long, electromagnetic (light) waves; often used in radio, TV, cell phone, and radar communication.

satellite A machine in space that sends information back and forth from Earth.

sensor An instrument that can detect changes in heat, sound, pressure, etc., and send the information to a machine.

Read More

Furstinger, Nancy. *Helper Robots.* Minneapolis: Lerner Publications Company, 2015.

Stewart, Melissa. *Robots.* Washington, D.C.: National Geographic, 2014.

Zuchora-Walske, Christine. *Weather Robots.* Minneapolis: Lerner Publications Company, 2015.

Websites

Drones to the Rescue
http://www.kidsdiscover.com/teacherresources/ drones-uavs-rescue/

Idaho Public Television Robotics
http://idahoptv.org/sciencetrek/topics/robots/index.cfm

NASA Robot Storybook
http://www.nasa.gov/audience/forstudents/k-4/ stories/ames-robot-storybook-text.html

Robots for Kids
http://sciencekids.co.nz/robots.html

Index

About the Author

Kirsten W. Larson is the author of more than 20 books for young readers. She used to work with rocket scientists at NASA, but now she writes about science for kids. Her favorite robots are NASA's *Curiosity* Mars Rover and LEGO Mindstorms. She lives near Los Angeles, California. Learn more at kirsten-w-larson.com.